SERMON ON THE MOUNT

JOHN STOTT

12 STUDIES
FOR INDIVIDUALS
OR GROUPS

ivp

Life
Builder
Study

INTER-VARSITY PRESS
36 Causton Street, London SW1P 4ST, England
Email: ivp@ivpbooks.com
Website: www.ivpbooks.com

Originally published in the United States of America in the LifeGuide® Bible Studies series
in 2000 by InterVarsity Press, Downers Grove, Illinois
First published in Great Britain by Scripture Union in 2000
Second edition published 2016
This edition published in Great Britain by Inter-Varsity Press 2018

British Library Cataloguing-in-Publication Data
A catalogue record for this book is available from the British Library.

ISBN: 978–1–78359–789–5

Printed in Great Britain by Ashford Colour Press Ltd, Gosport, Hampshire

Inter-Varsity Press publishes Christian books that are true to the Bible and that communicate
the gospel, develop discipleship and strengthen the church for its mission in the world.

IVP originated within the Inter-Varsity Fellowship, now the Universities and Colleges Christian
Fellowship, a student movement connecting Christian Unions in universities and colleges
throughout Great Britain, and a member movement of the International Fellowship of
Evangelical Students. Website: www.uccf.org.uk. That historic association is maintained,
and all senior IVP staff and committee members subscribe to the UCCF Basis of Faith.

Contents

Getting the Most Out of
Sermon on the Mount

The Sermon on the Mount is probably the best-known part of the teaching of Jesus, though arguably it is the least understood, and certainly it is the least obeyed. It is the nearest thing to a manifesto that he ever uttered, for it is his own description of what he wanted his followers to be and to do. The Sermon is found in Matthew's Gospel toward the beginning of Jesus' public ministry.

Immediately after his baptism and temptation Jesus had begun to announce the good news that the kingdom of God, long promised in the Old Testament era, was now on the threshold. He himself had come to inaugurate it. With him, the new age had dawned, and the rule of God had broken into history. "Repent," he cried, "for the kingdom of heaven is near" (Matthew 4:17). Indeed, "Jesus went throughout Galilee, teaching in their synagogues, preaching the good news of the kingdom" (Matthew 4:23).

The Sermon on the Mount, then, is to be seen in this context. It portrays the repentance (the Greek meaning is "the complete change of mind") and the righteousness which belong to the kingdom. That is, it describes what human life and human community look like when they come under the gracious rule of God. And what do they look like? Different! Jesus emphasized that his true followers, the citizens of God's kingdom, were to be entirely different from others. They were not to take their cue from the people around them, but from him, and so prove to be genuine children of their heavenly Father. To me the key text of the Sermon on the Mount is Matthew

6:8: "Do not be like them." It is immediately reminiscent of God's word to Israel in Leviticus 18:3: "You must not do as they do." It is the same call to be different. And right through the Sermon on the Mount this theme is elaborated.

Their character (the Beatitudes) was to be completely distinct from that admired by the world. They were to shine like lights in the prevailing darkness. Their righteousness was to exceed that of the scribes and Pharisees, both in ethical behavior and in religious devotion, while their love was to be greater and their ambition nobler than those of their pagan neighbors.

There is no single paragraph of the Sermon on the Mount where this contrast between Christian and non-Christian standards is not drawn. It is the underlying and uniting theme of the Sermon; everything else is a variation of it. Sometimes it is the Gentiles or pagan nations with which Jesus contrasts his followers. At other times he contrasts them with Jews. At all times Jesus teaches his followers are to be different—different from both the nominal church and the secular world, different from both the religious and the irreligious.

The Sermon on the Mount is the most complete description anywhere in the New Testament of the Christian counterculture. Here is a Christian value system, ethical standard, religious devotion, attitude to money, ambition, lifestyle and network of relationship—all of which are the total opposite of the non-Christian world. The Sermon presents life in the kingdom of God, a fully human life indeed but lived out under the divine rule.

Perhaps a majority of readers and commentators, looking the reality of human perversity in the face, have declared the standards of the Sermon on the Mount to be unattainable. Its ideals are noble but unpractical, they say, attractive to imagine but impossible to fulfill. At the other extreme are those superficial souls who glibly assert that the Sermon expresses ethical standards that are self-evidently true, common to all religions and easy to follow. "I live by the Sermon on the Mount," they say. The truth lies in neither extreme position. For the standards of the Sermon are neither readily attainable by everyone nor totally unattainable by anyone. To put them beyond anybody's reach is to ignore the purpose of Christ's Sermon; to put them within everybody's reach is to ignore the reality of our sin.

They are attainable all right, but only by those who have experienced the new birth that Jesus told Nicodemus was the indispensable condition of seeing and entering God's kingdom. For the righteousness he described in the Sermon is an inner righteousness. Although it manifests itself outwardly and visibly in words, deeds and relationships, it remains essentially a righteousness of the heart. Only a belief in the necessity and the possibility of a new birth can keep us from reading the Sermon on the Mount with either foolish optimism or hopeless despair. Jesus spoke the Sermon to those who were already his disciples and thereby also the citizens of God's kingdom and children of God's family. The high standards he set are appropriate only to such. We do not, indeed could not, achieve this privileged status by attaining Christ's standards. Rather by attaining his standards, or at least approximating them, we give evidence of what by God's free grace and gift we already are.

This Bible study draws on material first published in *The Message of the Sermon on the Mount*, a volume I have written in The Bible Speaks Today series (IVP). I recommend that book as supplementary reading for those using this guide. I am grateful to Jack Kuhatschek for the trouble he took and the skill he showed in preparing this guide under my general direction and to Donald Baker for making the necessary changes in this revised edition.

Those who first heard the Sermon on the Mount were astonished. I pray that you too will be astonished and challenged by the greatest sermon ever preached.

Suggestions for Individual Study

1. As you begin each study, pray that God will speak to you through his Word.

2. Read the introduction to the study and respond to the personal reflection question or exercise. This is designed to help you focus on God and on the theme of the study.

3. Each study deals with a particular passage—so that you can delve into the author's meaning in that context. Read and reread the passage to be studied. If you are studying a book, it will be helpful to read through the entire book prior to the first study. The questions are written using the language of the New International Version, so you may wish to use that version of the Bible. The New Revised Standard Version is also recommended.

4. This is an inductive Bible study, designed to help you discover for yourself what Scripture is saying. The study includes three types of questions. *Observation* questions ask about the basic facts: who, what, when, where and how. *Interpretation* questions delve into the meaning of the passage. *Application* questions help you discover the implications of the text for growing in Christ. These three keys unlock the treasures of Scripture.

Write your answers to the questions in the spaces provided or in a personal journal. Writing can bring clarity and deeper understanding of yourself and of God's Word.

5. It might be good to have a Bible dictionary handy. Use it to look up any unfamiliar words, names or places.

6. Use the prayer suggestion to guide you in thanking God for what you have learned and to pray about the applications that have come to mind.

7. You may want to go on to the suggestion under "Now or Later," or you may want to use that idea for your next study.

Suggestions for Members of a Group Study

1. Come to the study prepared. Follow the suggestions for individual study mentioned above. You will find that careful preparation will greatly enrich your time spent in group discussion.

2. Be willing to participate in the discussion. The leader of your group will not be lecturing. Instead, he or she will be encouraging the members of the group to discuss what they have learned. The leader will be asking the questions that are found in this guide.

3. Stick to the topic being discussed. Your answers should be based on the verses which are the focus of the discussion and not on outside authorities such as commentaries or speakers. These studies focus on a particular passage of Scripture. Only rarely should you refer to other portions of the Bible. This allows for everyone to participate in in-depth study on equal ground.

4. Be sensitive to the other members of the group. Listen attentively when they describe what they have learned. You may be surprised by their insights! Each question assumes a variety of answers. Many questions do not have "right" answers, particularly questions that aim at meaning or application. Instead the questions push us to explore the passage more thoroughly.

When possible, link what you say to the comments of others. Also, be affirming whenever you can. This will encourage some of the more hesitant members of the group to participate.

5. Be careful not to dominate the discussion. We are sometimes so eager to express our thoughts that we leave too little opportunity for others to respond. By all means participate! But allow others to also.

6. Expect God to teach you through the passage being discussed and through the other members of the group. Pray that you will have an enjoyable and profitable time together, but also that as a result of the study you will find ways that you can take action individually and/or as a group.

7. Remember that anything said in the group is considered confidential and should not be discussed outside the group unless specific permission is given to do so.

8. If you are the group leader, you will find additional suggestions at the back of the guide.

1

Unexpected Blessings

Matthew 5:1-12

A hymn by William Cowper reminds us to look for blessings in unexpected places.

> You fearful saints, fresh courage take;
> The clouds you so much dread
> Are big with mercy, and shall break
> In blessings on your head.

GROUP DISCUSSION. How would you define the word "blessed"? Ask each member of the group to write their definition on a piece of paper. Collect and read each definition, letting the group guess who wrote each one. What do the responses reveal about their authors?

PERSONAL REFLECTION. Who do you normally consider to be blessed or fortunate?

In the Beatitudes we find a simplicity of word and profundity of thought that has attracted each fresh generation of Christians and many others besides. The more we explore their implications, the more seems to remain unexplored. Their wealth is inexhaustible. Truly, "we are near heaven here." *Read Matthew 5:1-12.*

1. How does our normal description of the blessed or fortunate person compare with those Jesus considers blessed (vv. 1-12)?

2. To be "poor in spirit" (v. 3) is to acknowledge our spiritual poverty, our bankruptcy before God. Why is this an indispensable condition for receiving the kingdom of heaven?

Why is it so difficult for us to admit our spiritual poverty?

3. Why would those who are poor in spirit feel a need to mourn (v. 4)?

4. Those who mourn feel sorrow not only for their own sin but also for the sin they see around them. What have you heard in the news lately that causes you to mourn?

5. How do you think those who mourn will be comforted (v. 4)?

6. How would a true estimate of ourselves (vv. 3-4) lead us to be "meek"—to have a humble and gentle attitude to others (v. 5)?

7. From the world's point of view, why is it surprising that the meek will inherit the earth?

8. What has Jesus said so far that might lead us to hunger and thirst for righteousness (v. 6)?

9. Biblical righteousness has three aspects: legal, moral and social. What does it mean to hunger and thirst for each of these?

10. Jesus promises that those who hunger and thirst for righteousness will be filled (v. 6). What can you do to cultivate a healthy, hearty spiritual appetite?

Ask God to satisfy some of your hunger and thirst as you study the Sermon on the Mount.

Now or Later
Continue your study of the Sermon on the Mount focusing on verses 7-12.

---

11. Jesus says the merciful will be shown mercy (v. 7). Why do you think our treatment of others will affect God's treatment of us?

---

12. Why would the promise of seeing God (v. 8) be reserved for those who are pure in heart?

---

13. How can we be peacemakers (v. 9) in our homes, in our churches and in society?

---

14. Why would the world hate the kind of people described in the Beatitudes?

---

15. How have the Beatitudes challenged you to be different?

2

God's Way
to Make a Difference

Matthew 5:13-16

There are people in the world who never open a Bible. Still, they are forming impressions about God every time they meet a Christian. You may be the only Bible that someone will read.

GROUP DISCUSSION. Who has been like a Bible for you, showing in their life what God is like? What did that person say or do that showed God to you?

PERSONAL REFLECTION. In what ways have Christians had a positive influence on society?

What possible influence could the people described in the Beatitudes exert in this hard, tough world? What lasting good can the poor and the meek do, the mourners and the merciful—those who seek peace and not war? Would they not be overwhelmed by the flood of evil? What can they accomplish—whose only passion is righteousness and whose only weapon is purity of heart? Are not such people too feeble to achieve anything? Jesus does not share this skepticism, as this passage demonstrates. He expects us to have a profound influence on those around us. *Read Matthew 5:13-16.*

1. What positive qualities of salt and light do you think Jesus had in mind as he spoke these words?

2. Before refrigeration, salt was used to keep meat from rotting. What then does Jesus' statement "You are the salt of the earth" (v. 13) tell us about society and the church's role in it?

3. What has been in the news lately that indicates society is rotting and decaying?

4. What are some practical ways we can function as salt where we live and work (v. 13)?

5. What might cause Christians to lose their saltiness (v. 13)?

6. Jesus' second statement is "You are the light of the world" (v. 14). As salt we prevent decay, the spread of evil. How does the church's role as light complement its role as salt?

7. How can we positively promote the spread of truth in the world?

8. Why might we be tempted to hide our light (v. 15)?

9. What is the result, according to Jesus, of people seeing our good deeds (v. 16)?

10. What examples can you think of where the work of Christians has brought people closer to God?

11. What relationship do you see between the Beatitudes and our role as salt and light in society?

12. What is one way you can begin having a stronger influence as salt and as light?

Pray for the areas of rottenness in our world and for your ability to shine the light of truth.

Now or Later

Make plans with your small group (or on your own) to do a "salt and light" project. You could organize a clean up project in the city, serve in a soup kitchen, visit a nursing home or distribute Bibles in your dorm.

3

The Importance of Obeying God's Law

Matthew 5:17-20

John Wesley once wrote in his journal, "I am a Bible-bigot. I follow it in all things, both great and small."*

GROUP DISCUSSION. Do you agree with John Wesley? Should *everything* the Bible says still be followed today? Why or why not?

PERSONAL REFLECTION. If the Old Testament did not exist, what would be missing in your knowledge of God?

So far Jesus has spoken of the character of Christians. He has also emphasized the influence we will have in the world if we exhibit this character and if our character bears fruit in "good deeds." In Matthew 5:17-20 he proceeds to further define this character and these good deeds in terms of righteousness. This passage is of great importance not only for its definition of Christian righteousness but also for the light it throws on the relation between the New Testament and the Old Testament, between the gospel and the law. *Read Matthew 5:17-20.*

---

*Quoted in *Christianity Today* 40, no. 7.

1. This passage naturally divides into two parts, verses 17-18 and verses 19-20. What does each part emphasize?

2. Why might some people have thought that Jesus came to abolish the Law and the Prophets (v. 17)?

3. The Law and the Prophets (the Old Testament) consist of doctrine, prophecy and ethical precepts. In what sense has Jesus fulfilled each of these (v. 17)?

4. How does Jesus emphasize his high view of Old Testament Scripture (vv. 17-18)?

How can Jesus' words strengthen our confidence in Scripture?

---

5. What portions of the Bible have you tended to skip over or neglect?

How can you make studying these a higher priority?

---

6. How will our response to the Law determine our status in the kingdom of heaven (v. 19)?

---

7. The Pharisees and teachers of the law were zealous about observing the Law. How can our righteousness possibly surpass theirs (v. 20)?

8. Jesus states that only those who have this surpassing righteousness will enter the kingdom of heaven (v. 20). How can this be harmonized with his statement about the poor in spirit (those who admit their spiritual bankruptcy) entering the kingdom (5:3)?

9. Some people claim that Jesus abolished the law for the Christian and that we are only responsible for obeying the "law of love." Respond to this view in light of Jesus' words in this passage.

10. How should you study and apply the Old Testament law today?

Pray that you will receive new spiritual insight as you continue to study the Bible.

Now or Later

Take time to evaluate your life according to the Ten Commandments found in Exodus 20:1-17. Which of these have you been able to keep, and which do you struggle with? Spend time with God in confession and receive his forgiveness.

4

What's Wrong with Private Sins?

Matthew 5:21-30

Anger, rudeness and vengeance can often seem justified when we have been antagonized. Private thoughts of lust may seem harmless. Jesus, however, calls these attitudes "murder" and "adultery."

GROUP DISCUSSION. What advice would you give to someone who is struggling to get along with an irritating individual?

PERSONAL REFLECTION. In what ways has your thought life pleased or disappointed God this week?

The scribes and Pharisees calculated that the Law contained 248 commandments and 365 prohibitions. But they were better at arithmetic than obedience. So they tried to make the Law's demands less demanding and the Law's permissions more permissive. Throughout the Sermon on the Mount, Jesus seeks to reverse this tendency. He came to deepen, not destroy, the Law's demands. In this passage he explains the true meaning of the sixth and seventh commandments, the prohibitions against murder and adultery. *Read Matthew 5:21-30.*

1. What standard does Jesus use for determining right and wrong?

2. In verses 21-22 Jesus places murder and unrighteous anger in the same category. How are they related?

3. Jesus warns against calling someone *Raca* (an Aramaic word meaning "empty" or "stupid") or "You fool" (v. 22). Why do you think insults such as these constitute murder in God's sight?

4. What has caused you to lose your temper with people?

5. What do verses 23-26 teach us about broken relationships?

6. Why is Jesus concerned that reconciliation and apologies be made quickly?

7. When have you either initiated forgiveness or had someone initiate it with you?

What was the outcome?

8. What, according to Jesus, is the full meaning of the seventh commandment: "Do not commit adultery" (vv. 27-28)?

---

9. Lust has been compared to "a cannibal committing suicide by nibbling on himself."* How have you seen lust hurt yourself and others?

---

10. Some Christians have taken verses 29-30 literally and have mutilated their bodies. How do you think Jesus intends us to understand his warnings?

In what situations might you need to "gouge out an eye" or "cut off a hand"?

Ask God to help you rid your life of anything that causes you to sin. Pray that you will be able to obey him in your attitudes as well as your actions.

Now or Later

The subjects of anger and sexuality are also addressed in 1 Corinthians 6. What does this passage add regarding the need to settle disputes quickly? What does it teach about the dangers of lust? If there is someone you have not forgiven, go to that person now and seek reconciliation.

---

*Calvin Miller, "A Requiem for Love," *Christianity Today* 34, no. 2.

5

Faithfulness in Marriage & Speech

Matthew 5:31-37; 19:3-9

There is almost no unhappiness so painful as that of an unhappy marriage. And there is almost no tragedy as great as when a relationship God meant for love and fulfillment degenerates into a nonrelationship of bitterness, discord and despair.

GROUP DISCUSSION. Your group has been asked to write an article for *Good Partners magazine* entitled "The Top Ten Reasons Why Marriages Fail." What reasons will you give for the breakup of marriages?

PERSONAL REFLECTION. If you are married, ask God to use this study to give you some insight into your marriage. If you are single, ask God to use this study to help you encourage someone who is married.

Divorce is a controversial and complex subject that touches people's emotions at a deep level. Yet in spite of the painfulness of the subject, I am convinced that the teaching of Jesus on this and every subject is good—intrinsically good for individuals and for society. In this passage, Jesus calls us to faithfulness in marriage and honesty in speech. *Read Matthew 5:31-37 and 19:3-9.*

1. How do Jesus' statements contrast with the questions he was asked?

2. Rabbi Shammai taught that divorce was permitted only in extreme cases. Rabbi Hillel taught that it was permitted for any and every reason. How does this help us to understand the Pharisees' "test" question (19:3)?

3. Jesus points back to Genesis. What does this teach us about God's original design for marriage (19:4-6)?

4. How can you prepare for a marriage that meets God's original design?

What difference does God's design make in living as a married couple?

5. The Pharisees refer to Moses' instructions about divorce as a "command" (v. 7). What does Jesus' reply teach us about divorce (v. 8)?

In what ways might divorce reveal the hardness of our hearts?

6. What similarities and differences are there between 19:9 and 5:31-32?

How do these verses stress the seriousness of divorce?

7. How does Jesus' teaching contrast with today's views you and your peers have held concerning marriage and divorce?

8. *Read Matthew 5:33-37.* How might the issue of oaths and vows be connected to the topic of marriage and divorce?

9. The Pharisees had elaborate formulas for oaths, with some being binding and some not (see Matthew 23:16-22). Why is Jesus opposed to oaths?

10. Does this mean, for example, that we should refuse to give evidence under oath in a court of law? Explain.

---

11. Why should oaths be unnecessary for Jesus' followers?

Ask God to help you resist the pressures to compromise in marriage and in speech.

Now or Later

The group discussion topic was to create the article "The Top Ten Reasons Why Marriages Fail." Work now on the article "Top Ten Tips for a Strong Marriage."

If you are married, review the vows you have made with your spouse. Have you been faithful in keeping all the promises you made?

If you are unmarried, consider your present sexual behavior. What is your responsibility toward a future spouse?

6

How to Really Love Your Enemies

The real test of love does not come in how we relate to the kind and loveable but in how we relate to the cruel and despicable.

GROUP DISCUSSION. A friend keeps borrowing things from you but either fails to return them or returns them damaged. Confrontation has done no good. Do you (a) make the friend pay for anything lost or damaged, (b) refuse to loan anything else to your friend or (c) continue to loan anything he or she asks for? Explain.

PERSONAL REFLECTION. When have you found it difficult to forgive another person?

This passage brings us to the highest point of the Sermon on the Mount. Christ's words here are both most admired and most resented. He calls us to show our attitude of total love to an "evil person" (v. 39) and our "enemies" (v. 44). Nowhere is the challenge of the Sermon greater. Nowhere is the distinctness of the Christian counterculture more obvious. Nowhere is our need of the power of the Holy Spirit (whose first fruit is love) more compelling. *Read Matthew 5:38-48.*

1. What do you find most difficult about Jesus' instructions in these verses?

---

2. Jesus' quotation of "Eye for eye, and tooth for tooth" comes from Exodus 21:24. How would this instruction to Israel's judges clarify the meaning of justice?

How would it also limit the extent of revenge?

---

3. The Pharisees evidently extended this principle from the law courts (where it belonged) to the realm of personal relationships (where it did not belong). What consequences might have resulted?

---

4. Looking at verses 39-42, how would you contrast our natural responses in such situations with the responses Jesus expects of us?

---

5. What is accomplished by turning the other cheek or going a second mile?

---

6. In what situations might Christ's commands apply today?

7. According to Jesus, how are we to treat our enemies and why (vv. 44-45)?

—————————————————————————————————

8. In what ways is Jesus' command extraordinary (vv. 46-48)?

—————————————————————————————————

9. Does all this mean that Christians are to be doormats for the world to walk on? Explain.

—————————————————————————————————

10. How was Jesus himself an example of the principles "Do not resist an evil person" and "Love your enemies"?

—————————————————————————————————

11. How might you reflect your Father's character when you are mistreated?

Pray for God's blessing on people who have mistreated you or been your enemy.

Now or Later

Read Romans 13:1-5. How can we reconcile Christ's call to nonretaliation with the state's duty to punish evildoers?

7

How Not to Be Religious

Not conforming to the world is a familiar New Testament concept. But it is not so well known that Jesus also called us not to conform to the religious establishment. He saw (and foresaw) the worldliness of the nominal church and commanded the Christian community to be truly distinct from it in life and practice.

GROUP DISCUSSION. A friend that you invited to this Bible study has declined by saying that she finds all Christians to be hypocrites. What evidence is there that this is not true of the members of your group?

PERSONAL REFLECTION. Which of your words and actions might a person find hypocritical?

In Matthew 5 Jesus taught us that our righteousness must be greater than that of the Pharisees (because they obeyed the letter of the law, while our obedience must include our heart) and greater also than that of the pagans (because they love each other, while our love must include our enemies as well). Now in Matthew 6 Jesus draws the same two contrasts regarding our religion. He says that we should not be hypocritical like the Pharisees and not mechanical like the pagans. *Read Matthew 6:1-6 and 16-18.*

1. Jesus illustrates the principle of verse 1 by focusing on three religious practices: giving, praying and fasting. What images come to mind when you read about the hypocrites in verse 2?

2. In verse 1 Jesus commands us "not to do your 'acts of righteousness' before men, to be seen by them." Yet in 5:16 he said, "Let your light shine before men, so that they may see your good deeds." Is there a contradiction here? Explain.

3. What does Jesus mean when he says, "But when you give to the needy, do not let your left hand know what your right hand is doing" (v. 3)? Why is this important (vv. 2, 4)?

4. In what ways are we tempted to be hypocritical in our giving?

5. What was wrong with the way hypocrites prayed in Jesus' day (v. 5)?

6. In what ways do hypocrites pray today?

7. Why and how is our praying to be different (v. 6)?

8. How do you think the reward the Father will give us (v. 6) differs from the reward we receive from others (v. 5)?

_____

9. In verse 16 Jesus assumes Christians will fast (although few of us do). Why and how should we fast (vv. 16-18)?

_____

10. Fasting was a way that people were trying to seek the approval of others. In what other areas are we tempted to seek the approval of people rather than of God?

_____

11. How can this passage help to purify our motives?

Ask God to help you focus on him (rather than yourself) as you worship.

Now or Later

Read Luke 18:9-14. How does this story illustrate what Jesus teaches in Matthew 6?

When have you acted like the Pharisee in this story?

When have you acted like the tax collector?

8

A Pattern for Dynamic Prayer

Matthew 6:7-15

The fundamental difference between various kinds of prayer is the fundamentally different images of God that lie behind them.

GROUP DISCUSSION. Imagine that your prayers, like those in the Psalms, were recorded for others to read. What would people learn about your image of God?

PERSONAL REFLECTION. What are you pleased or encouraged about regarding your prayer life? What area do you struggle with?

The Lord's Prayer was given by Jesus as a model of what genuine Christian prayer should be like. According to Matthew he gave it as a pattern to copy ("This is how you should pray"), and according to Luke he gave it as an actual prayer ("When you pray, say . . ."). We are not obliged to choose, however, for we can both use the prayer as it stands and also model our own praying upon it. Either way, Jesus not only teaches us about prayer but also gives us a greater vision of the God we call "Our Father." *Read Matthew 6:7-15.*

---

1. What natural divisions do you observe in the Lord's Prayer? What is the focus of each?

2. How do pagan prayers (v. 7) differ from the persistent prayers Jesus himself offered (Matthew 26:44)?

3. In what ways might we be guilty of mindless, meaningless prayers?

4. If, as Jesus says in verse 8, God already knows what we need, why should Christians pray?

5. What does the phrase "Our Father in heaven" (v. 9) tell us about God?

6. What does it mean to "hallow" God's name (v. 9)?

7. God is already King. In what sense are his kingdom and perfect will still in the future (v. 10)?

8. In our self-centered culture we are often preoccupied with our own little name, empire and will rather than God's. How can we combat this tendency?

9. Some early commentators allegorized the word *bread* (v. 11), assuming that Jesus could not be referring to something as mundane as our physical needs. Why is it perfectly appropriate to pray for actual "daily bread"?

---

10. How is our heavenly Father's forgiveness related to our forgiving others (vv. 12, 14-15)?

---

11. If God cannot tempt us and trials are beneficial (James 1:2, 13), then what is the meaning of verse 13?

---

12. In what ways do your prayers need to more closely resemble this model prayer?

Take time now to pray, using the Lord's Prayer as your model.

Now or Later

The disciples whom Jesus trained to pray the Lord's Prayer later became great examples of prayer themselves. *Study one of their prayers in Acts 4:23-31.* What image of God is revealed in this prayer? How does this prayer resemble the Lord's Prayer? What further insights does this passage give for improving your prayer life?

9

What God Thinks of My Ambitions

Matthew 6:19-34

Everyone is ambitious to be or to do something. Childhood ambitions tend to follow certain stereotypes—to be an athlete, astronaut or movie star. Adults have their own narrow stereotypes too—to be wealthy, famous or powerful.

GROUP DISCUSSION. Share your childhood dreams. What did you want to be when you grew up? Why and how did this ambition change?

PERSONAL REFLECTION. What power has the spell of materialism held over you? How has it been hard to break?

Will Christian faith make a difference as you set your ambitions? In this passage Jesus helps us to choose well. He points out the folly of the wrong way and the wisdom of the right. Then he invites us to compare them and decide for ourselves. *Read Matthew 6:19-34.*

---

1. What, according to Jesus, are the most important things in life?

2. Why should we store up heavenly treasures rather than earthly ones (vv. 19-21)?

Does this mean that we cannot have personal property, savings accounts or insurance policies? Explain.

3. Practically speaking, how can we store up treasure in heaven?

4. How are physical and spiritual sight (or blindness) similar (vv. 22-23)?

5. Many people hold two jobs and are able to satisfy two bosses. So why would Jesus say that it is impossible to serve two masters—God and money (v. 24)?

6. How will the crucial choices we make in verses 19-24 affect our ability to live free from worry (v. 25)?

7. According to Jesus, why are we foolish to worry about our physical and material needs (vv. 25-30)?

8. How does worry also reveal a lack of faith (v. 30)?

9. If God promises to feed and clothe his children, then why are many of them ill-clad and undernourished (see Matthew 25:41-45)?

10. Give examples of how people today "run after all these things" that Jesus mentions (v. 32).

11. Why and how are our ambitions to be different from those of non-Christians (vv. 32-34)?

12. How has this passage challenged you to reexamine your goals and ambitions?

In prayer, talk with God over the issue of commitment. Will you hand over your priorities to him?

Now or Later

When Luke recorded the information we have just studied, he included an additional parable Jesus told about storing up treasure. *Read Luke 12:13-21.* Why did Jesus tell this parable?

In what ways is greed shown in people's lives?

Why did God call the rich man a fool?

How does a person become "rich toward God" (v. 21)?

10

Relationships That Encourage

The Christian community ought to be a supportive family where members are helping each other rise to higher degrees of righteousness, where relationships with God are being renewed and where unbelievers are being drawn to Christ. Unfortunately, it can also be a place where people feel condemned, manipulated and uncared for.

GROUP DISCUSSION. How has your church helped you grow closer to God? When has it failed to support you?

PERSONAL REFLECTION. Would people say that you have been an encouraging presence in the Christian community? Why or why not?

Matthew 7 may at first appear to be a series of self-contained paragraphs, but there is a connecting thread—relationships. The Christian counterculture is not an individualistic but a community affair, and relations both within the community and between the community and others are of paramount importance. *Read Matthew 7:1-12.*

1. What commands does Jesus make in these verses?

2. Why does Jesus tell us not to judge others (vv. 1-2)?

How do these verses expand on Jesus' statement about the merciful (5:7)?

---

3. According to Jesus, why are we often unfit to be judges (vv. 3-4)?

---

4. Some have assumed that Jesus was forbidding all judgment, even in law courts. How would you respond to this suggestion?

---

5. What steps must we take to truly help a brother or sister (v. 5)?

---

6. What kinds of people do you think he refers to as "dogs" and "pigs" (v. 6)?

7. Why is it futile, even dangerous, to talk with such people about the gospel?

8. What encouragement does Jesus give those who ask, seek and knock (vv. 7-8)?

How can we be assured of these promises (vv. 9-11)?

9. The Jewish Talmud states, "What is hateful to you, do not do to anyone else." Likewise, Confucius told his followers, "Do not to others what you would not wish done to you." How does the golden rule (v. 12) go beyond these commands?

In what sense does this rule sum up the Law and the Prophets?

10. Think of a relationship that is presently strained or broken. How can this passage help to mend that relationship?

What steps do you want to take this week?

Pray that in your relationships with other people you will grow as an encourager.

Now or Later

Further instruction about how we relate to other people is found in Romans 13:8-10. *Read this passage.* What debts does the author have in mind in verse 8?

Since we are not to use God's commands to judge and condemn each other, of what positive use can they be?

How would the "rule of love" apply to the relationship you thought about in question 10?

11

Detecting the Lies of Our World

Matthew 7:13-20

In our consumer-oriented society, people would like the opportunity to combine elements of several religions or even to design one of their own, but Jesus will not allow us this comfortable option. He insists that ultimately there is only one choice.

GROUP DISCUSSION. If God hired a consultant to help him improve his image among twenty-first-century Americans, what character qualities would the consultant want to emphasize? What changes might the consultant suggest God make in order to become more popular?

PERSONAL REFLECTION. Have you responded to the real God or to an image of who you would like him to be? How do you know the difference?

In the Sermon on the Mount the contrast between the two kinds of righteousness and devotion, the two treasures, the two masters and the two ambitions has been faithfully portrayed; now the time for decision has come. Is it to be the kingdom of Satan or the kingdom of God, the prevailing culture or the Christian counterculture? *Read Matthew 7:13-20.*

1. Why are broad gates and false prophets so appealing to people today?

2. How are the two gates described (vv. 13-14)?

3. In what sense is the gate of Christianity small and the road narrow?

4. In what sense is the world's gate wide and its road broad?

5. Why do you think many people dislike the notion that there is only one true gate?

6. Why is it significant that Jesus' warning about false prophets (vv.

15-20) comes immediately after his discussion of the narrow and wide gates?

7. Jesus says that false prophets "come to you in sheep's clothing" (v. 15). What disguises might they wear today (see vv. 21-23)?

8. What false messages or prophecies have you heard recently? How could you tell they were false?

9. In what sense are these false prophets like ferocious wolves?

10. Jesus also says, "By their fruit you will recognize them" (v. 16). What kind of fruit does he have in mind?

How can the quality of the fruit reveal the quality of the tree?

11. How can we keep from becoming "witch hunters" as we seek to recognize false prophets?

12. "Every tree that does not bear good fruit is cut down and thrown into the fire" (v. 19). How can this warning to false prophets also keep us from becoming complacent as Christians?

Pray that you will know the truth and have the courage to enter through the narrow gate.

Now or Later

Anyone claiming to teach spiritual truth will attempt to answer certain basic questions such as:

Goal: If you succeed perfectly in your ideology or religion, what will you attain?

Diagnosis: What is wrong with humanity (or the world)?

Means: How do you propose to attain your goal?

Decide how you would answer each of these questions. Compare your answers to other beliefs you have studied. Knowing what the Bible teaches is the best defense against false prophets.

12

Making the Choice of a Lifetime

The most momentous decision a person will ever make—more than the choice of a career or life-partner—is the choice about life itself. How will I react to Jesus?

GROUP DISCUSSION. If during a discussion about different religions a friend says, "Well, at least we're all headed for the same place," how would you reply?

PERSONAL REFLECTION. On what basis do you expect to enter the kingdom of heaven?

The two final paragraphs of the Sermon are very similar. Both contrast the wrong and the right responses to Christ's teaching. Both show that neutrality is impossible and that a definite decision has to be made. Both stress that nothing can take the place of an active, practical obedience. And both teach that the issue of life and death on the day of judgment will be determined by our moral response to Christ and his teaching in this life. *Read Matthew 7:21-29.*

---

1. Describe the various types of people Jesus talks about in these verses. How does each respond to Jesus' teaching?

2. On the surface, what might we admire about those described in verses 21-23?

---

3. In spite of their admirable statements or actions, why does Jesus condemn such people?

---

4. Why do people so often confuse religious activity with doing the will of the father?

How do you understand the difference?

---

5. How were the two houses similar and different (vv. 24-27)?

---

6. Why is it often difficult to tell the difference between genuine Christians and counterfeit ones?

---

7. How did the storms reveal what was previously unseen?

8. What kinds of storms have you faced in life? What did they reveal about the quality of your life?

---

9. The crowds were amazed at Jesus' teaching, because he taught as one who had authority (vv. 28-29). In what ways was Jesus' authority demonstrated in his Sermon?

---

10. What difference does it make to you that Jesus taught with authority (v. 29)?

---

11. How do verses 21-29 provide a fitting conclusion to the Sermon on the Mount?

---

12. What are some of the "words" of Jesus you have heard in the Sermon on the Mount (v. 24) that you want to have stick with you?

Ask the Lord to help you submit to his authority, especially in those areas where you feel disobedient or hypocritical.

Now or Later
Think of one teaching from the Sermon that has challenged you most. How can you begin putting it into practice?

Leader's Notes

MY GRACE IS SUFFICIENT FOR YOU. (2 COR 12:9)

Leading a Bible discussion can be an enjoyable and rewarding experience. But it can also be *scary*—especially if you've never done it before. If this is your feeling, you're in good company. When God asked Moses to lead the Israelites out of Egypt, he replied, "O Lord, please send someone else to do it"! (Ex 4:13). It was the same with Solomon, Jeremiah and Timothy, but God helped these people in spite of their weaknesses, and he will help you as well.

You don't need to be an expert on the Bible or a trained teacher to lead a Bible discussion. The idea behind these inductive studies is that the leader guides group members to discover for themselves what the Bible has to say. This method of learning will allow group members to remember much more of what is said than a lecture would.

These studies are designed to be led easily. As a matter of fact, the flow of questions through the passage from observation to interpretation to application is so natural that you may feel that the studies lead themselves. This study guide is also flexible. You can use it with a variety of groups—student, professional, neighborhood or church groups. Each study takes forty-five to sixty minutes in a group setting.

There are some important facts to know about group dynamics and encouraging discussion. The suggestions listed below should enable you to effectively and enjoyably fulfill your role as leader.

Preparing for the Study

1. Ask God to help you understand and apply the passage in your own life. Unless this happens, you will not be prepared to lead others. Pray too for the various members of the group. Ask God to open your hearts to the message of his Word and motivate you to action.

2. Read the introduction to the entire guide to get an overview of the entire book and the issues which will be explored.

3. As you begin each study, read and reread the assigned Bible passage to familiarize yourself with it.

4. This study guide is based on the New International Version of the Bible. It will help you and the group if you use this translation as the basis for your study and discussion.

5. Carefully work through each question in the study. Spend time in meditation and reflection as you consider how to respond.

6. Write your thoughts and responses in the space provided in the study guide. This will help you to express your understanding of the passage clearly.

7. It might help to have a Bible dictionary handy. Use it to look up any unfamiliar words, names or places. (For additional help on how to study a passage, see chapter five of *How to Lead a LifeBuilder Study*, IVP, 2018.)

8. Consider how you can apply the Scripture to your life. Remember that the group will follow your lead in responding to the studies. They will not go any deeper than you do.

9. Once you have finished your own study of the passage, familiarize yourself with the leader's notes for the study you are leading. These are designed to help you in several ways. First, they tell you the purpose the study guide author had in mind when writing the study. Take time to think through how the study questions work together to accomplish that purpose. Second, the notes provide you with additional background information or suggestions on group dynamics for various questions. This information can be useful when people have difficulty understanding or answering a question. Third, the leader's notes can alert you to potential problems you may encounter during the study.

10. If you wish to remind yourself of anything mentioned in the leader's notes, make a note to yourself below that question in the study.

Leading the Study

1. Begin the study on time. Open with prayer, asking God to help the group to understand and apply the passage.

2. Be sure that everyone in your group has a study guide. Encourage the group to prepare beforehand for each discussion by reading the introduction to the guide and by working through the questions in the study.

3. At the beginning of your first time together, explain that these studies are meant to be discussions, not lectures. Encourage the members of the to participate. However, do not put pressure on those who may be hesitant to speak during the first few sessions. You may want to suggest the following guidelines to your group.

☐ Stick to the topic being discussed.

☐ Your responses should be based on the verses which are the focus of the discussion and not on outside authorities such as commentaries or speakers.

☐ These studies focus on a particular passage of Scripture. Only rarely should you refer to other portions of the Bible. This allows for everyone to participate in in-depth study on equal ground.

☐ Anything said in the group is considered confidential and will not be discussed outside the group unless specific permission is given to do so.

☐ We will listen attentively to each other and provide time for each person present to talk.

☐ We will pray for each other.

4. Have a group member read the introduction at the beginning of the discussion.

5. Every session begins with a group discussion question. The question or activity is meant to be used before the passage is read. The question introduces the theme of the study and encourages group members to begin to open up. Encourage as many members as possible to participate, and be ready to get the discussion going with your own response.

This section is designed to reveal where our thoughts or feelings need to be transformed by Scripture. That is why it is especially important not to read the passage before the discussion question is asked. The passage will tend to color the honest reactions people would otherwise give because they are, of course, supposed to think the way the Bible does.

You may want to supplement the group discussion question with an icebreaker to help people to get comfortable. See the community section of the *Small Group Starter Kit* (IVP, 1995) for more ideas.

You also might want to use the personal reflection question with your group. Either allow a time of silence for people to respond individually or discuss it together.

6. Have a group member (or members if the passage is long) read aloud the passage to be studied. Then give people several minutes to read the passage again silently so that they can take it all in.

7. Question 1 will generally be an overview question designed to briefly survey the passage. Encourage the group to look at the whole passage, but try to avoid getting sidetracked by questions or issues that will be addressed later in the study.

8. As you ask the questions, keep in mind that they are designed to be used just as they are written. You may simply read them aloud. Or you may prefer to express them in your own words.

There may be times when it is appropriate to deviate from the study guide. For example, a question may have already been answered. If so, move on to the next question. Or someone may raise an important question not covered in the guide. Take time to discuss it, but try to keep the group from going off on tangents.

9. Avoid answering your own questions. If necessary, repeat or rephrase them until they are clearly understood. Or point out something you read in the leader's notes to clarify the context or meaning. An eager group quickly becomes passive and silent if they think the leader will do most of the talking.

10. Don't be afraid of silence. People may need time to think about the question before formulating their answers.

11. Don't be content with just one answer. Ask, "What do the rest of you think?" or "Anything else?" until several people have given answers to the question.

12. Acknowledge all contributions. Try to be affirming whenever possible. Never reject an answer. If it is clearly off-base, ask, "Which verse led you to that conclusion?" or again, "What do the rest of you think?"

13. Don't expect every answer to be addressed to you, even though this will probably happen at first. As group members become more at ease, they will begin to truly interact with each other. This is one sign of healthy discussion.

14. Don't be afraid of controversy. It can be very stimulating. If you don't resolve an issue completely, don't be frustrated. Move on and keep it in mind for later. A subsequent study may solve the problem.

15. Periodically summarize what the group has said about the passage. This helps to draw together the various ideas mentioned and gives continuity to the study. But don't preach.

16. At the end of the Bible discussion you may want to allow group members a time of quiet to work on an idea under "Now or Later." Then discuss what you experienced. Or you may want to encourage group members to work on these ideas between meetings. Give an opportunity during the session for people to talk about what they are learning.

17. Conclude your time together with conversational prayer, adapting the prayer suggestion at the end of the study to your group. Ask for God's help in following through on the commitments you've made.

18. End on time.

Many more suggestions and helps are found in *How to Lead a LifeBuilder Study*.

Components of Small Groups

A healthy small group should do more than study the Bible. There are four components to consider as you structure your time together.

Nurture. Small groups help us to grow in our knowledge and love of God. Bible study is the key to making this happen and is the foundation of your small group.

Community. Small groups are a great place to develop deep friendships with other Christians. Allow time for informal interaction before and after each study. Plan activities and games that will help you get to know each other. Spend time having fun together—going on a picnic or cooking dinner together.

Worship and prayer. Your study will be enhanced by spending time praising God together in prayer or song. Pray for each other's needs—and keep track of how God is answering prayer in your group. Ask God to help you to apply what you are learning in your study.

Outreach. Reaching out to others can be a practical way of applying what you are learning, and it will keep your group from becoming self-focused. Host a series of evangelistic discussions for your friends or neighbors. Clean up the yard of an elderly friend. Serve at a soup kitchen together, or spend a day working in the community.

Many more suggestions and helps in each of these areas are found in the *Small Group Starter Kit*. You will also find information on building a small group. Reading through the starter kit will be worth your time.

Study 1. Unexpected Blessings.
Matthew 5:1-12.

Purpose: To see that we receive blessings as we live out Christian character.

Question 1. This Bible study draws on material first published in *The Message of the Sermon on the Mount*, a volume I have written in The Bible Speaks Today series (IVP). I recommend that book as supplementary reading, especially for the person leading the study.

The Greek word *makarios* can and does mean "happy." So J. B. Phillips translates the opening words of each Beatitude "How happy are . . . !" And several commentators have described the Beatitudes as Jesus' prescription for human happiness. Nevertheless it is seriously misleading to render *makarios* "happy." For happiness is a subjective state, whereas Jesus is making an objective judgment about these people. He is declaring not what they may feel like ("happy"), but what God thinks of them and what on that account they are ("blessed").

Question 2. The poverty and hunger to which Jesus refers in the Beatitudes are spiritual states. It is true that the Aramaic word Jesus used may have been simply "poor," as in Luke's version (Lk 6:20-23). But then "the poor," God's poor, were already a clearly defined group in the Old Testament, and Matthew will have been correct to translate "poor in spirit." For "the poor" were not so much the poverty stricken as the pious who—partly because they were needy, downtrodden, oppressed or in other ways afflicted—had put their faith and hope in God.

Question 3. One might almost translate this second beatitude "Happy are the unhappy" in order to draw attention to the startling paradox it contains. It is plain from the context that those here promised comfort are not primarily those who mourn the loss of a loved one but those who mourn the loss of their innocence, their righteousness, their self-respect. It is not the sorrow of bereavement to which Christ refers but the sorrow of repentance.

Question 5. Such mourners who bewail their own sinfulness will be comforted by the only comfort that can relieve their distress, namely, the free forgiveness of God. According to the Old Testament, Messiah was to be "the Comforter" who would "bind up the brokenhearted" (Is 61:1-3). And Christ does pour oil into our wounds and speak peace to our sore, scarred consciences. Yet we still mourn over the havoc of suffering and death that sin spreads throughout the world. For only in the final state of glory will Christ's comfort be complete; for only then will sin be no more, and "God will wipe away every tear from their eyes" (Rev 7:17).

Question 6. We tend to think of "the meek" as weak and effeminate. Yet the Greek adjective means "gentle," "humble," "considerate" and "courteous." Dr. Lloyd-Jones sums it up admirably: "Meekness is essentially a true view of oneself, expressing itself in attitude and conduct with respect to others. . . . The man who is truly meek is the one who is truly amazed that God and man can think of him as well as they do and treat him as well as they do." (*Studies in the Sermon on the Mount* [Leicester, England: Inter-Varsity Press, 1977], pp. 68-69).

Question 7. The godless may boast and throw their weight about, yet real possession eludes their grasp. The meek, on the other hand, although they may be deprived and disenfranchised by humanity, yet because they know what it is to live and reign with Christ, can enjoy and even "possess" the earth, which belongs to Christ. Then on the day of "the regeneration" there will be "new heavens and a new earth" for them to inherit. Thus the way of Christ is different from the way of the world, and all Christians, even if they are like Paul in "having nothing," can yet describe themselves as "possessing everything." As Rudolf Stier put it, "Self-renunciation is the way to world-dominion" (*The Words of the Lord Jesus,* [T & T Clark, 1874], p. 105).

Question 9. Legal righteousness is justification, a right relationship with God. Moral righteousness is that righteousness of character and conduct which pleases God. Social righteousness, as we learn from the Law and the Prophets, is concerned with seeking humanity's liberation from oppression, together with the promotion of civil rights, justice in the law courts, integrity in business dealings, and honor in home and family affairs.

Question 10. Luther expressed this concept with his customary vigor: "The command to you is not to crawl into a corner or into the desert, but to run out, if that is where you have been, and to offer your hands and your feet and your whole body, and to wager everything you have and can do." What is required, he goes on, is "a hunger and thirst for righteousness that can never be curbed or stopped or sated, one that looks for nothing and cares for nothing except the accomplishment and maintenance of the right, despising everything that hinders this end. If you cannot make the world completely pious, then do what you can." (*The Sermon on the Mount,* trans. Jaroslav Pelikan, Luther's Work, Vol. 21 [St. Louis: Concordia, 1956] p. 27).

Study 2. God's Way to Make a Difference. Matthew 5:13-16.
Purpose: To consider the kind of influence Jesus expects us to have on those around us.

Question 2. Notice that questions 2-5 look at our role as salt, while questions 6-10 look at our role as light. Then questions 11-12 draw the two together. God has established certain institutions in his common grace, which curb our selfish tendencies and prevent society from slipping into anarchy. Chief among these are the state (with its authority to frame and enforce laws) and the home (including marriage and family life). These exert a wholesome influence in the community. Nevertheless, God intends the most powerful of all restraints within sinful society to be his own redeemed, regenerate and righteous people. As R. V. G. Tasker puts it, the disciples are "to be a moral disinfectant in a world where moral standards are low, constantly changing, or nonexistent" (*The Gospel According to St. Matthew,* Tyndale New Testament Commentary [Leicester, England: Inter-Varsity Press, 1961], p. 63).

Question 5. Strictly speaking, salt can never lose its saltiness. But Dr. David Turk has suggested to me that what was then popularly called "salt" was in fact a white powder (perhaps from around the Dead Sea) which, while containing sodium chloride, also contained much else, since in those days there were no refineries. Of this dust the sodium chloride was probably the most soluble component and so the most easily washed out. The residue of white powder still looked like salt, and was doubtless still called salt, but it neither tasted nor acted like salt. It was just road dust.

Question 6. The effects of salt and light are complementary. The function of salt is largely negative: it prevents decay. The function of light is positive: it illumines the darkness. For it is one thing to stop the spread of evil; it is another to promote the spread of truth, beauty and goodness. Jesus calls us to do both.

Question 8. We may be tempted to hide our light because we are afraid of the people who hate light and what they might do. We may also be embarrassed, timid or unaware of opportunities.

Question 9. Jesus says we give light by our "good deeds." It seems that "good deeds" is a general expression to cover everything Christians say and do because they are Christians, every outward and visible manifestation of their Christian faith. They express not only our loyalty to God but also our care for others as well. Indeed, the primary meaning of "deeds" must be practical, visible acts of compassion. It is when people see these, Jesus said, that they will glorify God, for they embody the good news of his love, which we proclaim. Without them our gospel loses its credibility and our God his honor.

Question 11. A Christian's character as described in the Beatitudes and a Christian's influence as defined in the salt and light metaphors are related to one another. Our influence depends on our character.

Study 3. The Importance of Obeying God's Law. Matthew 5:17-20.
Purpose: To understand the meaning of Christian righteousness and the place of Scripture in our lives.

Question 1. If the group has some trouble with this question, you might ask them to look at the pronouns to see if this sheds any light on the different emphasis of each part. Verses 17-18 discuss Christ and the law, while 19-20 focus on the Christian and the law.

Question 2. Jesus spoke with his own authority. He loved to use a formula no ancient prophet or modern scribe had ever used, "Truly I say to you," speaking in his own name and with his own authority. What was this authority of his? Was he setting himself up as an authority against the sacred law, the Word of God? So it seemed to some. Hence their question, spoken or unspoken, Jesus now answered unequivocally: "Do not think that I have come to abolish the Law or the Prophets."

Question 3. The verb translated "to fulfill" (*plerosai*) means literally "to fill" and indicates, as Chrysostom expressed it, that "his [Christ's] sayings were no repeal of the former, but a drawing out and filling up of them." Christ fulfilled the doctrinal teaching of the Old Testament by bringing its partial revelation to completion by his person, his teaching and his work. He fulfilled predictive prophecy because what was predicted about the Messiah came to pass in him. And he fulfilled the ethical precepts of the Old Testament by obeying them and giving us their true interpretation. The group might also discuss how Jesus fulfilled the ceremonial laws, including the priesthood and sacrifices.

Question 4. The "smallest letter" of the Hebrew alphabet was a *yod*, almost as small as a comma. The "least stroke of a pen" probably refers to one of the tiny hooks or projections that distinguished some Hebrew letters from others. Jesus' reference now was only to "the Law" rather than to "the Law and the Prophets" as in the previous verse, but we have no reason to suppose that he was deliberately omitting the Prophets; "the Law" was a comprehensive term for the total divine revelation of the Old Testament. None of it will pass away or be discarded, he says, not a single letter or part of a letter, until it has all been fulfilled. And this fulfillment will not be complete until the heaven and the earth themselves pass away.

Question 6. There is a vital connection between the law of God and the kingdom of God. Because Jesus has come not to abolish but to fulfill and because not an iota or dot will pass from the law until all has been fulfilled, *therefore* greatness in the kingdom of God will be measured by conformity to it. Nor is personal obedience enough; Christian disciples must also teach to others the permanently binding nature of the law's commandments. True, not all the commandments are equally "weighty." Yet even *one of the least of these commandments*, precisely because it is a commandment of God the King, is important. To relax it—that is, to loosen its hold on our conscience and its authority in our life—is an offense to God whose law it is. To disregard a "least" commandment in the law (in either obedience or instruction) is to demote oneself into a "least" subject in the kingdom; greatness in the kingdom belongs to those who are faithful in doing and teaching the whole moral law.

Question 7. Our Lord's statement in verse 20 must certainly have astonished his first hearers as it astonishes us today. But Christian righteousness far surpasses pharisaic righteousness in kind rather than in degree. It is not so much that Christians succeed in keeping 240 commandments when the best Pharisees may only have scored 230. No, Christian righteousness is greater than pharisaic righteousness because it is deeper, being a righteousness of the heart. The scribes and Pharisees were actually attempting (according to Jesus) to make Old Testament commands more manageable and less exacting by describing in tortuous detail what it actually meant to obey particular laws. Jesus sought to reverse this. As we will see in the six "You have heard it said" passages (see vv. 21, 27, 31, 33, 38, 43) to be discussed in the next three studies, Jesus is preaching a much more demanding interpretation of Scripture than even the Pharisees. Because this may not become clear to the group during this study, you may want to ask them to hold their questions until you have had a chance to finish studying Matthew 5.

Question 8. People can have the "surpassing righteousness" when they are committed to God's law with their mind and motive and yet be "poor in spirit" when they recognize how far they are from their (and God's) ideal.

Question 9. The apostle Paul summarizes the "law of love" in Galatians 5:14, "The entire law is summed up in a single command: 'Love your neighbor as yourself.'" However, some people mistakenly assume that if our actions are motivated by love, then we can do whatever we wish—even those things that are contrary toward the law. In every generation of the Christian era there have been those who could not accommodate themselves to Christ's attitude toward the law. The famous second-century heretic Marcion, who rewrote the New Testament by eliminating its references to the Old, naturally erased this passage. Some of his followers went even further. They dared even to reverse its meaning by exchanging the verbs so that the sentence read: "I have come not to fulfill the law and the prophets, but to abolish them"! Their counterparts today seem to be those who have embraced the so-called new morality. They regard the law as rigid and authoritarian, and (just like the Pharisees) they attempt to "relax" its authority, to loosen its hold. So they declare the category of law abolished (which Jesus said he had not come to abolish) and they set law and love at variance with each other (in a way in which Jesus never did). No, Jesus disagreed with the Pharisees' interpretation of the law; he never disagreed with their acceptance of its authority. Rather the reverse. In the strongest possible terms he asserted its authority as God's written Word, and called his disciples to accept its true and deeply exacting interpretation.

Study 4. What's Wrong with Private Sins? Matthew 5:21-30.

Purpose: To understand how anger and lust are related to the commandments against murder and adultery.

Question 1. In order to make obedience more readily attainable, the Pharisees restricted the commandments and extended the permissions of the law.

They made the law's demands less demanding and the law's permissions more permissive. What Jesus did was to reverse both tendencies. He insisted instead that the full implications of God's commandments must be accepted without imposing any artificial limits, whereas the limits that God had set to his permission must also be accepted and not arbitrarily increased.

Question 2. Verse 21 is not a prohibition against taking all human life in any and every circumstance. This is clear from the fact that the same Mosaic law, which forbids killing in the Decalogue, elsewhere calls for it both in the form of capital punishment and in the wars designed to exterminate the corrupt pagan tribes that inhabited the Promised Land.

Question 3. The scribes and Pharisees were evidently seeking to restrict the application of the sixth commandment to the deed of murder alone, the act of spilling human blood in homicide. If they refrained from this, they considered that they had kept the commandment. And this apparently is what the rabbis taught the people. But Jesus disagreed with them. The true application of the prohibition was much wider, he maintained. It included thoughts and words as well as deeds, anger and insult as well as murder. Not all anger is evil, as is evident from the wrath of God, which is always holy and pure. And even fallen human beings may sometimes feel righteous anger, although, being fallen, we should ensure that even this is slow to rise and quick to die down (Jas 1:19; Eph 4:26, 27). The reference of Jesus, then, is to unrighteous anger, the anger of pride, vanity, hatred, malice and revenge.

Question 5. In these verses Jesus proceeds to give a practical application of the principles he has just enunciated. His theme is that if anger and insult are so serious and so dangerous, then we must avoid them at all cost and take action as speedily as possible. We must never allow an estrangement to remain, still less to grow. We must not delay to put it right. If we want to avoid committing murder in God's sight, we must take every possible positive step to live in peace and love with all people.

Question 6. The need for quick action is related to the seriousness of the offense. If murder is a horrible crime, malicious anger and insult are horrible too. And so is every deed, word, look or thought by which we hurt or offend a fellow human being.

Question 8. There is not the slightest suggestion here that natural sexual relations within the commitment of marriage are anything but God-given and beautiful. We may thank God that the Song of Solomon is contained in the canon of Scripture, for there is no Victorian prudery there but rather the uninhibited delight of lovers, of bride and bridegroom in each other. No, the teaching of Jesus here refers to unlawful sex outside marriage, whether practiced by married or unmarried people. Similarly, Jesus' allusion is to all forms of immorality. To argue that the reference is only to a man lusting after a woman and not vice versa, or only to a married man and not an unmarried man, since the offender is said to commit "adultery," not "fornication," is to be guilty of the very sin that Jesus was condemning in the Pharisees. His emphasis is that any and every sexual practice which is immoral in deed is immoral also in look and thought.

Question 10. On the surface it is a startling command to pluck out an offending eye, to cut off an offending hand or foot. A few Christians whose zeal greatly exceeded their wisdom have taken Jesus literally. The best known example is the third-century scholar Origen of Alexandria, who actually made himself a eunuch. Not long after, in A.D. 325, the Council of Nicea was right to forbid this barbarous practice. The command to get rid of troublesome eyes, hands and feet is an example of our Lord's use of dramatic figures of speech. What he was advocating was not a literal physical self-maiming but a ruthless moral self-denial. Not mutilation but mortification is the path of holiness he taught, and mortification or "taking up the cross" to follow Christ means to reject sinful practices so resolutely that we die to them or put them to death (see Mk 8:34; Rom 8:13; Gal 5:24; Col 3:5).

Question 11. To obey this command of Jesus will involve for many of us a certain "maiming." We shall have to eliminate from our lives certain things that (though some may be innocent in themselves) either are, or could easily become, sources of temptation. In this metaphorical language we may find ourselves without eyes, hands or feet. That is, we shall deliberately decline to read certain literature, see certain films, visit certain exhibitions. If we do this, we shall be regarded by some of our contemporaries as narrow-minded, untaught Philistines. "What?" they will say to us incredulously, "you've not read such and such a book? You've not seen such and such a film? Why, you're not educated, man!" They may be right. We may have had to become culturally "maimed" in order to preserve our purity of mind. The only question is whether, for the sake of this gain, we are willing to bear that loss and endure that ridicule.

Study 5. Faithfulness in Marriage & Speech. Matthew 5:31-37; 19:3-9.
Purpose: To consider why we should be faithful in marriage and honest in speech.

Question 1. The Pharisees' question was so framed as to draw Jesus out on what he considered to be legitimate grounds for divorce. For what cause might a man divorce his wife? For one cause or several causes or any cause? Jesus' reply was not a reply. He declined to answer their question. Instead, he asked a counter-question about their reading of Scripture.

Question 2. The debate between Rabbi Shammai and Rabbi Hillel centered on the interpretation of Deuteronomy 24:1-4, especially the phrase "he finds something indecent about her" (v. 1). Rabbi Shammai took a rigorist line and taught that something indecent referred to some grave matrimonial offense. Rabbi Hillel, on the other hand, interpreted this phrase in the widest possible way to include a wife's most trivial offenses. If she proved to be an incompetent cook and burned her husband's food, or if he lost interest in her because of her plain looks and because he became enamored with some other more beautiful woman, these things were "something indecent" and justified his divorcing her. The Pharisees seem to have been attracted by Rabbi Hillel's laxity, which explains the form of their question: "Is it lawful for a man to divorce his wife for any and every reason?" In other words they wanted to know whose side Jesus was on in the contemporary debate, and whether he belonged to the school of rigorism or of laxity.

Question 3. The Pharisees were preoccupied with the grounds for divorce; Jesus with the institution of marriage. He referred them back to Genesis, both to the creation of humanity as male and female (Gen 1) and to the institution of marriage (Gen 2) by which a man leaves his parents and cleaves to his wife and the two become one. This biblical definition implies that marriage is both exclusive ("a man . . . his wife") and permanent ("be united" to his wife). It is these two aspects of marriage that Jesus selects for emphasis in his comments which follow.

Marriage, according to our Lord's exposition of its origins, is a divine institution by which God makes permanently one two people who decisively and publicly leave their parents in order to form a new unit of society and then "become one flesh."

Question 5. The Pharisees emphasized the giving of a divorce certificate, as if this were the most important part of the Mosaic provision, and then referred to both the certificate and the divorce as "commands" of Moses. But a careful reading of Deuteronomy 24:1-4 reveals something quite different. To begin with, the whole paragraph hinges on a long series of conditional clauses. This may be brought out in the following paraphrase: "After a man has married a wife, if he finds something indecent in her, and if he gives her a certificate of divorce and divorces her and she leaves, and if she marries again, and if her second husband gives her a certificate of divorce and divorces her, or if her second husband dies, then her first husband who divorced her is forbidden to remarry her." The thrust of the passage is to prohibit remarriage to one's own divorced partner. The reason for this regulation is obscure. For our purposes here it is enough to observe that this prohibition is the only command in the whole passage; there is certainly no command to a husband to divorce his wife, nor even any encouragement to do so. All there is, instead, is a reference to certain necessary procedures if a divorce takes place; and therefore at the very most a reluctant permission is implied and a current practice is tolerated. Yet even the divine concession was in principle inconsistent with the divine institution of marriage, as Jesus points out in 19:8. If you are able to control discussion enough so that too much time is not taken up here, you might want to have the group turn to Deuteronomy 24:1-4. But if your group is talkative, you might just want to summarize what is mentioned above if it would be helpful in your discussion. An unwillingness or inability to forgive a marriage partner and be reconciled might reveal how hardened we are by sin to the grace and mercy of God.

Question 6. Jesus allows only one exception to the rule that remarriage after divorce results in adultery. That is the so-called exception clause in 5:32 and 19:9: "except for marital unfaithfulness." Conservative scholars disagree about why it is omitted from the parallel passages in Mark and Luke. They also disagree about the meaning of "marital unfaithfulness" *(porneia)*. It seems likely that its absence from Mark and Luke is due not to their ignorance of it but to their acceptance of it as something taken for granted. After all, under the Mosaic law adultery was punishable by death (although the death penalty for this offense seems to have generally fallen into disuse by the time of Jesus), so nobody would have questioned that marital unfaithfulness was a just ground for divorce. Even the rival Rabbis Shammai and Hillel were agreed about this. The Greek word for "marital unfaithfulness" is normally translated "fornication," denoting the immorality of the unmarried and is often distinguished from adultery, the immorality of the married.

For this reason some have argued that the exception clause permits divorce if some premarital sexual sin is later discovered. But the Greek word is not precise enough to be limited in this way. It is derived from *porne*, "prostitute," without specifying whether she (or her client) is married or unmarried. Further, it is used in the Septuagint for the unfaithfulness of Israel, Yahweh's bride, as exemplified in Hosea's wife, Gomer. It seems, therefore, that we must agree with R. V. G. Tasker's conclusion that *porneia* is "a comprehensive word, including adultery, fornication and unnatural vice" (*The Gospel According to St. Matthew*, Tyndale New Testament Commentaries [Grand Rapids, Mich.: Eerdmans, 1961], p. 184).

Question 9. Verse 33 is not an accurate quotation of any one law of Moses.

At the same time, it is an accurate summary of several Old Testament precepts that require people who make vows to keep them. These include Exodus 20:7, Leviticus 19:12, Numbers 30:2 and Deuteronomy 23:21. The Pharisees got to work on these awkward prohibitions and tried to restrict them. They shifted people's attention away from the vow itself and the need to keep it to the formula used in making it. Jesus teaches that a vow is binding irrespective of its accompanying formula. That being so, the real implication of the law is that we must keep our promises and be people of our word. Then vows become unnecessary.

Question 10. The Anabaptists took this line in the sixteenth century and most Quakers still do today. While admiring their desire not to compromise, one can still perhaps question whether their interpretation is not excessively literalistic. Jesus emphasized in his teaching that honest people do not need to resort to oaths; he did not say they should refuse to take an oath if required by some external authority to do so.

Question 11. Question 9 concerns the negative effects of oaths. This question covers why oaths aren't needed (even if there were no harmful aspects to them). As Christians, our simple answers should carry all the weight needed to convince people that we are honest and reliable, that we will follow through on what we promise. People should be able to trust us because of our character rooted in Christ.

Study 6. How to Really Love Your Enemies. Matthew 5:38-48.

Purpose: To learn how and why we should love our enemies.

Question 2. This principle was also stated in Leviticus 24:20 and Deuteronomy 19:21. The context makes it clear beyond question that this was an instruction to the judges of Israel. Indeed, they are mentioned in Deuteronomy 19:17-18. It expressed the principle of an exact retribution whose purpose was both to lay the foundation of justice, specifying the punishment that a wrong doer deserved, and to limit the compensation of his victim to an exact equivalent and no more. It is almost certain that by the time of Jesus literal retaliation for damages had been replaced in Jewish legal practice by money penalties or "damages." Indeed, there is evidence of this much earlier. Exodus 21:26-27 states that if a man strikes his slave so as to destroy his eye or knock out his tooth, instead of losing his own eye or tooth (which he would deserve but which would be no compensation to the disabled slave), he must lose his slave: "He must let the servant go free to compensate for the eye [or tooth]." We may be quite sure that in other cases too this penalty was not physically exacted, except in the case of murder ("life for life"); it was commuted to a payment of damages.

Question 3. The scribes and Pharisees tried to use this principle to justify personal revenge, although the law explicitly forbade this: "Do not seek revenge or bear a grudge against one of your people, but love your neighbor as yourself" (Lev 19:18). Thus, "this excellent, if stern, principle of judicial retribution was being utilized as an excuse for the very thing it was instituted to abolish, namely personal revenge" (John W. Wenham, *Christ and the Bible* [Downers Grove, Ill.: InterVarsity Press, 1972], p. 35).

Question 5. The true value of this command is in what it does for the person who turns the other cheek. As an example, consider Martin Luther King Jr. At his funeral, Dr. Benjamin Mays commented: "If any man knew the meaning of suffering, King knew. House bombed; living day by day for thirteen years under constant threats of death; maliciously accused of being a Communist; falsely accused of being insincere . . . ; stabbed by a member of his own race; slugged in a hotel lobby; jailed over twenty times; occasionally deeply hurt because friends betrayed him—and yet this man had no bitterness in his heart, no rancor in his soul, no revenge in his mind; and he went up and down the length and breadth of this world preaching non-violence and the redemptive power of love." (Coretta Scott King, *My Life with Martin Luther King Jr.* (Hodder & Stoughton, 1970), pp. 365-69).

Question 7. We are told to love our enemies with both service and words. The point Jesus is making is that true love is not sentiment so much as service—practical, humble, sacrificial service. As Dostoyevsky put it somewhere, "Love in action is much more terrible than love in dreams." Our enemies seek our harm; we must seek their good. For this is how God has treated us. It is "while we were enemies" that Christ died for us to reconcile us to God. If he gave himself for his enemies, we must give ourselves for ours.

Words can also express our love, however, both words addressed to our enemies themselves and words addressed to God on their behalf. "Bless those who curse you." If they call down disaster and catastrophe upon our heads, expressing in words their wish for our downfall, we must retaliate by calling down heaven's blessing upon them, declaring in words that we wish them nothing but good.

Question 8. Divine love is indiscriminate love, shown equally to good people and bad. But all human love, even the highest, the noblest and the best, is contaminated to some degree by the impurities of self-interest. We Christians are specifically called to love our enemies (in which love there is no self-interest), and this is impossible without the supernatural grace of God. If we love only those who love us, we are no better than swindlers. If we greet only our brothers and sisters, our fellow Christians, we are no better than pagans; they too greet one another. The question Jesus asked is: *What more are you doing than others?* (47). This simple word *more* is the quintessence of what he is saying. It is not enough for Christians to *resemble* non-Christians; our calling is to outstrip them in virtue.

Question 9. Christ does not intend for his followers to be doormats. His illustrations and personal example depict not the weakling who offers no resistance. He himself challenged the high priest when questioned by him in court (Jn 18:19-23). And the apostle Paul once "resisted" (same Greek word) the apostle Peter to his face (Gal 2:11-14). They depict rather the strong man whose control of himself and love for others are so powerful that he rejects absolutely every conceivable form of retaliation. The only limit to the Christian's generosity will be a limit that love itself might impose. So the command of Jesus not to resist evil should not properly be used to justify either temperamental weakness, political anarchy or even total pacifism. Instead, what Jesus here demands of all his followers is a personal attitude to evildoers that is prompted by mercy not justice, renounces retaliation so completely as to risk further costly suffering, is never governed by the desire to cause them harm but always by the determination to serve their highest good.

Question 10. It had been written of Jesus in the Old Testament: "I offered my back to those who beat me, my cheeks to those who pulled out my beard; I did not hide my face from mocking and spitting" (Is 50:6). And in the actual event the Jewish police spat on him, blindfolded him and struck him in the face, and then the Roman soldiers followed suit. They crowned him with thorns, clothed him in the imperial purple, invested him with a scepter of reed, jeered at him, "Hail, King of the Jews," knelt before him in mock homage, spat in his face and struck him with their hands (Mk 14:65; 15:16-20). And Jesus, with the infinite dignity of self-control and love, held his peace. He demonstrated his total refusal to retaliate by allowing them to continue their cruel mockery until they had finished.

Question 11. The Christian's righteousness, whether expressed in purity, honesty or charity, will show to whom we belong. Our Christian calling is to imitate not the world but the Father. And it is by this imitation of him that the Christian counterculture becomes visible. Some holiness teachers have built upon verse 48 great dreams of the possibility of reaching in this life a state of sinless perfection. But the words of Jesus cannot be pressed into meaning this without causing discord in the Sermon. For he has already indicated in the Beatitudes that a hunger and thirst after righteousness is a perpetual characteristic of his disciples, and in the next chapter he will teach us to pray constantly, "Forgive us our debts" (6:12). Both the hunger for righteousness and the prayer for forgiveness, being continuous, are clear indications that Jesus did not expect his followers to become morally perfect in this life. The context shows that the "perfection" he means relates to love, the perfect love of God that is shown even to those who do not return it. We are to love our enemies with the merciful, inclusive love of God.

Study 7. How Not to Be Religious. Matthew 6:1-6, 16-18.

Purpose: To consider proper and improper motives for our religious conduct.

Question 1. The three illustrations follow an identical pattern. In vivid and deliberately humorous imagery, Jesus paints a picture of the hypocrite's way of being religious. It is the way of ostentation. Such receive the reward they want, the applause of others. With this he contrasts the Christian way, which is secret, and the only reward that Christians want, the blessing of God who is their heavenly Father and who sees in secret. Taking time to picture the scenes Jesus is painting will help bring home the vividness of his comments to his original hearers—and to us as well.

Question 2. Verses 7-15 will be covered in the next study. The discrepancy is only verbal, not substantial. The clue lies in the fact that Jesus is speaking against different sins. It is our human cowardice which made him say, "Let your light shine before men," and our human vanity which made him tell us to beware of practicing our piety before men. A. B. Bruce sums it up well when he writes that we are to "show when tempted to hide" and "hide when tempted to show" (*Commentary on the Synoptic Gospels, The Expositor's Greek Testament*, ed. W. Robertson Nicholl [London: Hodder, 1897], p. 116). Our good works must be public so that our light shines; our religious devotions must be secret lest we boast about them.

Question 3. The question is not so much what the hand is doing (giving over some cash or writing a check) but what the heart is thinking while the hand is doing it.

Question 5. There was nothing wrong in standing to pray, for this was the usual posture for prayer among the Jews. Nor were they necessarily mistaken to pray on the street corners as well as in the synagogues if their motive was to break down segregated religion and bring their recognition of God out of the holy places into the secular life of everyday. But Jesus uncovered their true motive as they stood in synagogue or street with hands uplifted to heaven in order that they might be seen by others. Behind their piety lurked their pride. What they really wanted was applause. They got it. "They have received their reward in full." Rather than becoming absorbed in the mechanics of secrecy, we need to remember that the purpose of Jesus' emphasis on "secret" prayer is to purify our motives in praying.

Question 7. Jesus said, "Go into your room and shut the door." We are to close the door against disturbance and distraction but also to shut out the prying eyes of men and to shut ourselves in with God. Only then can we obey the Lord's next command: *Pray to your Father who is in secret*, or as the Jerusalem Bible clarifies it, 'who is in that secret place'. Our Father is there, waiting to welcome us. Just as nothing destroys prayer like side glances at human spectators, so nothing enriches it like a sense of the presence of God. For he sees not the outward appearance only but the heart, not the one who is praying only but the motive for which he prays. The essence of Christian prayer is to seek God.

Question 8. R. V. G. Tasker points out that the Greek word for the "room" into which we are to withdraw to pray *(tameion)* "was used for the storeroom where treasures might be kept." The implication may be, then, that "there are treasures already awaiting" us when we pray (*Matthew*, p. 73). Certainly the hidden rewards of prayer are too many to enumerate. In the words of the apostle Paul, when we cry, "Abba, Father," the Holy Spirit witnesses with our spirit that we are indeed God's children, and we are granted a strong assurance of his fatherhood and love (Rom 5:5; 8:16). He lifts the light of his face upon us and gives us his peace (Num 6:26). He refreshes our soul, satisfies our hunger, quenches our thirst. We know we are no longer orphans, for the Father has adopted us; no longer prodigals, for we have been forgiven; no longer alienated, for we have come home.

Question 9. Strictly speaking, fasting is a total abstention from food. It can be legitimately extended, however, to mean going without food partially or totally, for shorter or longer periods. There can be no doubt that in Scripture fasting has to do in various ways with self-denial and self-discipline. First and foremost, to "fast" and to "humble ourselves before God" are virtually equivalent terms (Ps 35:13; Is 58:3, 5). Sometimes this was an expression of penitence for past sins. When people were deeply distressed over their sin and guilt, they would both weep and fast (Neh 9:1-2; Dan 9:2-19; 10:2-3; Jon 3:5; Acts 9:9). We are not to humble ourselves before God only in penitence for past sin, however, but also in dependence on him for future mercy. For if penitence and fasting go together in Scripture, "prayer and fasting" are even more often coupled (Ex 24:18; 2 Chron 20:1-4; Ezra 8:21-23; Esther 4:16; Mt 4:1-2; Acts 13:1-3; 14:23). Our fasting can also be a means of self-discipline. A voluntary abstinence from food is one way of increasing our self-control (1 Cor 9:24-27). Likewise, fasting can be a deliberate doing without in order to share what we might have eaten (or its cost) with the undernourished (Is 58:1-7).

Question 11. Although one of the refrains of this passage is "before men in order to be seen and praised by men," it is not men with whom the hypocrite is obsessed but himself. "Ultimately," writes Dr. Lloyd-Jones, "our only reason for pleasing men around us is that we may please ourselves." (*Studies in the Sermon on the Mount* [Downers Grove, Ill.: InterVarsity Press, 1977], p. 330). The remedy then is obvious. We have to become so conscious of God that we cease to be self-conscious. And it is on this that Jesus concentrates.

Study 8. A Pattern for Dynamic Prayer. Matthew 6:7-15.

Purpose: To learn how we should pray.

Question 1. In the first part of this question you are simply looking for what verses are covered in each half of the Lord's Prayer: verses 9-10 and 11-13. Then, in the second part of the question look for the subject of each half. If the group needs help, tell them to notice that in the second half of the Lord's Prayer the possessive adjective changes from "your" to "our," as we turn from God's affairs to our own. The well-known phrase "for yours is the kingdom and the power and the glory forever" is not found in the earliest manuscripts.

Question 2. Jesus is not condemning perseverance in prayer but rather verbosity, especially in those who speak without thinking.

Question 4. Believers do not pray to God to tell him things he doesn't know or to motivate him to keep his promises or to urge him to do what he really doesn't want to do at all. Rather, prayer is for our benefit—to exercise our faith and to cast our worries on him. As Luther put it in his commentary on this passage, "By our praying . . . we are instructing ourselves more than we are him."

Question 5. The words "in heaven" denote not the place of God's abode so much as the authority and power at his command as the creator and ruler of all things. Thus he combines fatherly love with heavenly power, and what his love directs his power is able to perform.

Question 6. The name of God is not a combination of the letters G, O and D. The name stands for the person who bears it, for his character and activity. So God's "name" is God himself as he is in himself and has revealed himself. His name is already holy in that it is separate from and exalted over every other name. But we pray that it may be hallowed, ("treated as holy"), because we ardently desire that due honor may be given to it, that is to him whose name it is, in our own lives, in the church and in the world.

Question 7. The kingdom of God is his royal rule. Again, as he is already holy so he is already King, reigning in absolute sovereignty over both nature and history. Yet when Jesus came he announced a new and special break-in of the kingly rule of God, with all the blessings of salvation and the demands of submission that the divine rule implies. To pray that his kingdom may "come" is to pray both that it may grow, as through the church's witness people submit to Jesus, and that soon it will be consummated when Jesus returns in glory to take his power and reign.

Question 8. You might ask the group to think of situations in which we could demonstrate greater concern for God's name than our name, God's kingdom than our "kingdom" and God's will than our will.

Question 9. Early church fathers like Tertullian, Cyprian and Augustine thought the reference was either to "the invisible bread of the Word of God" (Augustine) or to the Lord's Supper. Jerome, in the Vulgate, translated the Greek word for "daily" by the monstrous adjective "supersubstantial"; he also meant the Holy Communion. A more ordinary, down-to-earth interpretation seems most likely—just as the Lord daily provided manna for the Israelites in the desert (Ex 16:4).

Question 10. Jesus certainly does not mean that our forgiveness of others earns us the right to be forgiven. Rather he means that God forgives only the penitent and that one of the chief evidences of true penitence is a forgiving spirit. Once our eyes have been opened to see the enormity of our offense against God, the injuries which others have done to us appear by comparison extremely trifling. If, on the other hand, we have an exaggerated view of the offenses of others, it proves that we have minimized our own.

Question 11. It is probable that the prayer is more that we may overcome temptation, than that we may avoid it. Perhaps we could paraphrase the whole request as, "Do not allow us so to be led into temptation that overwhelms us, but rescue us from the evil one." So behind these words that Jesus gave us to pray are the implications that the devil is too strong for us, that we are too weak to stand up to him, but that our heavenly Father will deliver us if we call on him.

Study 9. What God Thinks of My Ambitions. Matthew 6:19-34.

Purpose: To learn why we should not be ambitious for material security but rather for God's rule.

Question 2. What Jesus forbids his followers is the selfish accumulation of goods ("Do not store up for yourselves treasures on earth"): extravagant and luxurious living, the hard-heartedness that does not feel the colossal need of the world's underprivileged people, the foolish fantasy that a person's life consists in the abundance of his or her possessions, and the materialism that tethers our hearts to the earth. In other words to store up treasure on earth does not mean being provident (making sensible provision for the future) but being covetous (like misers who hoard and materialists who always want more). This is the real snare of which Jesus warns here.

Question 3. What are "treasures in heaven"? Jesus does not explain. Yet surely we may say that to "store up" treasures in heaven is to do anything on earth whose effects last for eternity. Encourage the group to think of several examples.

Question 4. Not infrequently in Scripture the "eye" is equivalent to the "heart." That is, to "set the heart" and to "fix the eye" on something are synonyms. Therefore, Jesus' argument seems to go like this: just as our eye affects our whole body, so our ambition (where we fix our eyes and heart) affects our whole life.

Question 5. A supervisor usually only places limited demands on the employee (for example, to work a certain number of hours a week). Thus a person could satisfy two bosses if the hours required by each do not conflict. But Jesus is referring to slave owners who own "all" of a slave. Thus it is impossible to be owned completely by two masters.

Question 6. It is a pity that this passage is often read on its own, isolated from what has gone before. Then the significance of the introductory "Therefore I tell you" (v. 25) is missed. So we must relate this "therefore," this conclusion of Jesus, to the teaching that has led up to it. He calls us to thought before he calls us to action. He invites us to look clearly and coolly at the alternatives before us and to weight them carefully. Only when we have grasped with our minds the comparative durability of the two treasures, the comparative usefulness of the two eye conditions and the comparative worth of the two masters, are we ready to consider Jesus' words: "Therefore I tell you" this is how you must go on to behave.

Question 7. An exclusive preoccupation with food, drink and clothing could be justified only if physical survival were the be-all and end-all of existence. We just live to live. Then indeed how to sustain the body would be our proper first concern. So it is understandable that in emergency famine conditions the struggle to survive must take precedence over other things. But for this to be so in ordinary circumstances would express a reductionist concept of humanity that is totally unacceptable. It would downgrade us to the level of animals, indeed to that of birds and plants. Yet the great majority of today's advertisements are directed toward the body—underwear to display it at its shapeliest, deodorants to keep it smelling sweet and alcoholic beverages to pep it up when it is languishing. This preoccupation prompts these questions: is physical well-being a worthy object to devote our lives to? Has human life no more significance than this? *The Gentiles seek all these things.* Let them. But as for you, my disciples, Jesus implies, they are a hopelessly unworthy goal. For they are not the "Supreme Good" in life.

Questions 8-9. The Lord promises that our heavenly Father can be trusted to feed and clothe us. Yet even faithful believers are not exempt from the following: First, believers are not exempt from earning their own living. We cannot sit back in an armchair, twiddle our thumbs, mutter "my heavenly Father will provide" and do nothing. We have to work. As Paul put it later: "If a man will not work, he shall not eat" (2 Thess 3:10). Second, believers are not exempt from responsibility for others. It seems significant that in this same Gospel of Matthew the Jesus who says that our heavenly Father feeds and clothes his children later says that we must ourselves feed the hungry and clothe the naked, and will be judged accordingly (Mt 25:31-46). Third, believers are not exempt from experiencing trouble. Jesus forbids his people to worry. But freedom from worry and freedom from trouble are not the same thing. At the end of this paragraph the reason Jesus gives why we are not to worry about tomorrow is: "Each day has enough trouble of its own." So then, God's children are promised freedom neither from work, nor from responsibility, nor from trouble, but only from worry. Worry is incompatible with Christian faith.

Question 11. Ambitions for self may be quite modest (enough to eat, to drink and to wear, as in the Sermon) or they may be grandiose (a bigger house, a faster car, a higher salary, a wider reputation, more power). But whether modest or immodest, these are ambitions for myself—*my* comfort, *my* wealth, *my* status, *my* power.

Ambitions for God, however, if they are to be worthy, can never be modest. There is something inherently inappropriate about cherishing small ambitions for God. How can we ever be content that he should acquire just a little more honor in the world? No. Once we are clear that God is King, then we long to see him crowned with glory and honor, and accorded his true place, which is the supreme place. We become ambitious for the spread of his kingdom and righteousness everywhere.

Study 10. Relationships That Encourage. Matthew 7:1-12.
Purpose: To describe the quality of relationships the Father desires for his children.
Question 2. The simple but vital point that Jesus is making in these verses is

that we are not God. No human being is qualified to be the judge of others, for we cannot read each other's hearts or assess each other's motives. Not only are we not the judge, but we are among the judged and shall be judged with the greater strictness ourselves if we dare to judge others.

Question 3. The picture of somebody struggling with the delicate operation of removing a speck of dirt from a friend's eye while a vast plank in his own eye entirely obscures his vision is ludicrous. Yet when the caricature is transferred to ourselves and our ridiculous fault finding, we do not always appreciate the joke. We have a fatal tendency to exaggerate the faults of others and minimize the gravity of our own.

Question 4. The context does not refer to judges in courts of law but rather to the responsibility of individuals to one another. Likewise, our Lord's injunction to "judge not" cannot be understood as a command to suspend our critical faculties in relation to other people, to turn a blind eye to their faults (pretending not to notice them), to avoid all criticism and to refuse to discern between truth and error, goodness and evil. Much of Christ's teaching in the Sermon on the Mount is based on the assumption that we will (indeed should) make value judgments. If, then, Jesus was neither abolishing law courts nor forbidding criticism, what did he mean by "Do not judge"? It is not a requirement to be blind but rather a plea to be generous. Jesus does not tell us to cease to be human (by suspending our critical powers which help to distinguish us from animals) but to renounce the presumptuous ambition to be God (by setting ourselves up as judges).

Question 5. Again it is evident that Jesus is not condemning criticism as such but rather the criticism of others when we exercise no comparable self-criticism, nor correction as such but rather the correction of others when we have not first corrected ourselves.

Question 6. By giving them these names Jesus is indicating not only that they are more animals than humans but that they are animals with dirty habits as well. The dogs he had in mind were not the well-behaved lapdogs of an elegant home but the wild pariah dogs, vagabonds and mongrels, which scavenged in the city's rubbish dumps. And pigs were unclean animals to the Jew —not to mention their love for mud. The apostle Peter later referred to them by bringing together two proverbs: "A dog returns to its vomit" and "A sow that is washed goes back to her wallowing in the mud" (2 Pet 2:22). So then, the "dogs" and "pigs" with whom we are forbidden to share the gospel pearl are not just unbelievers. They must rather be those who have had ample opportunity to hear and receive the good news, but have decisively—even defiantly—rejected it. We cheapen God's gospel by letting them trample it under foot. At the same time, to give people up is a very serious step to take.

Question 8. All three verbs are present imperatives and indicate the persistence with which we should make our requests known to God. The force of Jesus' parable (vv. 9-11) lies in a contrast rather than a comparison between God and humanity. It is another *a fortiori* or "how much more" argument: if human parents (although evil) know how to give good gifts to their children, how much more will our heavenly Father (who is not evil but wholly good) give good gifts to those who ask him (v. 11).

Question 9. Not doing hateful acts is one thing (the Talmud and Confucius). Positively seeking someone's good is another (Jesus). Self-advantage often guides us in our own affairs; now we must also let it guide us in our behavior to others. All we have to do is use our imagination, put ourselves in the other person's shoes and ask, "How would I like to be treated in that situation?" If someone asks about the Talmud, you can tell them that it is a collection of ancient rabbinic writings that form the basis of religious authority for traditional Judaism.

Study 11. Detecting the Lies of Our World. Matthew 7:13-20.

Purpose: To see the importance of entering the narrow gate and of watching out for those who teach otherwise.

Question 2. This is a simple observation question, so feel free to move quickly to the next question after people have had a chance to answer. What is immediately striking about these verses is the absolute nature of the choice before us. We would all prefer to be given many more choices than only one, or better still to fuse them all into a conglomerate religion and thus eliminating the need for any choice. But Jesus cuts across our easy going syncretism. He will not allow us the comfortable solutions we propose. Instead he insists that ultimately there is only one choice because there are only two possibilities from which to choose. There are two gates, two roads, two destinations and two groups. We must choose one or the other; we cannot be neutral.

Question 3. The narrowness of the road is due to divine revelation that restricts pilgrims to the confines of what God has revealed in Scripture to be true and good. Revealed truth imposes a limitation on what Christians may believe, and revealed goodness on how we may behave.

Question 4. On the broad road there is plenty of room for diversity of opinions and laxity of morals. It is the road of tolerance and permissiveness. It has no curbs, no boundaries of either thought or conduct. Travelers on this road follow their own inclinations, that is, the desires of the human heart in its fallenness. Superficiality, self-love, hypocrisy, mechanical religion, false ambition, censoriousness—these things do not have to be learned or cultivated. Effort is needed to resist them. No effort is required to practice them. That is why the broad road is easy.

Question 6. One of the major characteristics of false prophets in the Old Testament was their amoral optimism which insisted that God's way was really the broad way. They denied that God was the God of judgment as well as steadfast love and mercy. False prophets give a false sense of security. They lull people to sleep in their sins. They fail to warn people of the impending judgment of God or tell them how to escape it.

Questions 7-9. False prophets are adept at blurring the issue of salvation. Some so muddle or distort the gospel that they make it hard for seekers to find the narrow gate. Others try to make out that the narrow way is in reality much broader than Jesus implied, and that to walk it requires little if any restriction on one's belief or behavior. Yet others dare to contradict Jesus and assert that the broad road does not lead to destruction but that, as a matter of fact, all roads lead to God, and that even the broad and narrow roads, although they lead off in opposite directions, ultimately both end in life. No wonder Jesus likened such false teachers to ferocious wolves. They are responsible for leading people to the very destruction which they say does not exist.

Question 10. A prophet's "fruit" is not only character and manner of life. Indeed, interpreters "who confine them to the life are, in my opinion, mistaken," wrote Calvin. A second fruit is the person's actual teaching. This is strongly suggested by the other use Jesus made of the same fruit-tree metaphor: "A tree is recognized by its fruit. You brood of vipers, how can you who are evil say anything good? For out of the overflow of the heart the mouth speaks. The good man brings good things out of the good stored up in him, and the evil man brings evil things out of the evil stored up in him" (Mt 12:33-35). So then, if our hearts are revealed in our words, as a tree is known by its fruit, we have a responsibility to test teachers by their teaching.

Question 11. The application of the "fruit" test is not altogether simple or straightforward. For fruit takes time to grow and ripen. We have to wait for it patiently. We also need an opportunity to examine it closely, for it is not always possible to recognize a tree and its fruit from a distance. Indeed, even at close quarters we may at first miss the symptoms of disease in the tree or the presence of a maggot in the fruit. To apply this to a teacher, what is needed is not a superficial estimate of his standing in the church but a close and critical scrutiny of his character, conduct, message, motives and influence.

Study 12. Making the Choice of a Lifetime. Matthew 7:21-29.

Purpose: To decide on which foundation we are going to build our lives.

Question 1. In this passage Jesus sets before us the radical choice between obedience and disobedience, and calls us to an unconditional commitment of mind, will and life to his teaching. The way he does it is to warn us of two unacceptable alternatives, first a merely verbal profession (vv. 21-23) and secondly a merely intellectual knowledge (vv. 24-27). Neither can be a substitute for obedience; indeed each may be camouflage for disobedience.

Question 2. The kind of Christian profession Jesus describes at the end of the Sermon appears—at least on the surface—to be wholly admirable. To begin with, it is polite. It addresses him as "Lord," just as today the most respectful and courteous way of referring to Jesus is still to say "our Lord." Next, the profession is orthodox. Although to call Jesus "Lord" may mean no more than "Sir," the present context contains allusions both to God as his Father and to himself as the Judge, and therefore seems to imply more. Thirdly, it is fervent, for it is not a cold or formal "Lord" but an enthusiastic "Lord, Lord," as if the speaker wishes to draw attention to the strength and zeal of his devotion. The forth point is that it is a public confession. This is no private and personal protestation of allegiance to Jesus. Some have even "prophesied" in Christ's name, daring to claim as they preach on some public occasion the authority and the inspiration of Jesus himself.

Question 3. The reason Jesus rejects these people is that their profession was verbal, not moral. It concerned their lips only, and not their life. They called Jesus "Lord, Lord," but never submitted to his lordship or obeyed the will of his heavenly Father. The reason Christ the Judge will banish them from him is that they are evildoers. They may claim to do mighty works in their ministry, but in their everyday behavior the works they do are not good but evil.

Question 4. We who claim to be Christians in our day have made a profession of faith in Jesus privately in conversion and publicly in baptism or confirmation. We appear to honor Jesus by referring to him as "the Lord" or "our Lord." We recite the creed in church and sing hymns expressive of devotion to Christ. We even exercise a variety of ministries in his name. But he is not impressed by our pious and orthodox words. He still asks for evidence of our sincerity in good works of obedience.

Question 5. A casual observer would not have noticed any difference between the two houses. For the difference was in the foundations, and foundations are not seen.

Questions 7-8. The real question is not whether we hear Christ's teaching (or even whether we respect or believe it) but whether we do what we hear. Only a storm will reveal the truth. Sometimes a storm of crisis or calamity betrays what manner of person we are, for "true piety is not fully distinguished from its counterfeit till it comes to the trial" (Bruce, *Synoptic Gospels,* p. 135). If not, the storm of the Day of Judgment will certainly do so.

Questions 9-10. Jesus' hearers naturally compared and contrasted him with the many other teachers with whom they were familiar, especially the scribes. What struck them most was that he taught them "as one who had authority, and not as their teachers of the law." For the teachers of the law claimed no authority of their own. They conceived their duty in terms of faithfulness to the tradition they had received. So they delved into commentaries, searching for precedents, claiming the support of famous names among the rabbis. Their only authority lay in the authorities they were constantly quoting. Jesus, on the other hand, had not received a scribal education, scandalized the establishment by sweeping away the traditions of the elders, had no particular reverence for social conventions and spoke with a freshness of his own that captivated some and infuriated others. A. B. Bruce summed up the difference by saying that the scribes spoke "by authority," while Jesus spoke "with authority" (*Synoptic Gospels,* p. 136). If he did not teach like the teachers of the law, he did not teach like the Old Testament prophets either. The most common formula with which the prophets introduced their oracles, namely, "Thus says the Lord," is one Jesus never used. Instead, he would begin, "Truly, truly, I say to you," thus daring to speak in his own name and with his own authority, which he knew to be identical with the Father's.

John Stott is known worldwide as a preacher, evangelist and communicator of Scripture. Stott has written many books, including Basic Christianity *and* Basic Christian Leadership, *He has also written the LifeBuilder Bible Study* The Cross.